POPULAR SONGS

HAL LEONARD
STUDENT PIANO LIBRARY

Classic Christmas Favorites

Arranged by Jennifer and Mike Watts

CONTENTS

ISBN 978-1-4803-9489-6

HAL•LEONARD®
CORPORATION

7777 W. BLUEMOUND RD. P.O. BOX 13819 MILWAUKEE, WI 53213

Visit Hal Leonard Online at
www.halleonard.com

All I Want for Christmas Is My Two Front Teeth

Words and Music by
Don Gardner
Arranged by Jennifer and Mike Watts

"Sis-ter Su-sie sit-ting on a this-tle!" Gosh, oh gee, how hap-py I'd be, if

I could on-ly whis-tle (thhh). All I want for Christ-mas is my two front teeth, my

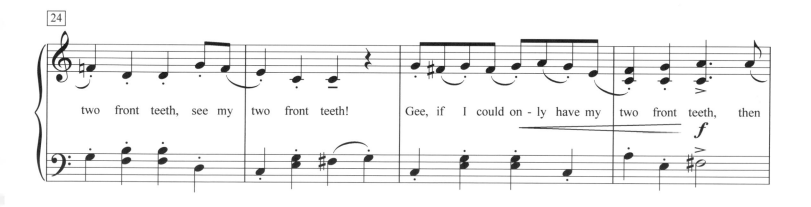

two front teeth, see my two front teeth! Gee, if I could on-ly have my two front teeth, then

I could wish you, "Mer-ry... I could wish you, "Mer-ry Christ-mas!"

I'll Be Home for Christmas

Words and Music by Kim Gannon
and Walter Kent
Arranged by Jennifer and Mike Watts

find me   where the love - light gleams.   I'll   be home for

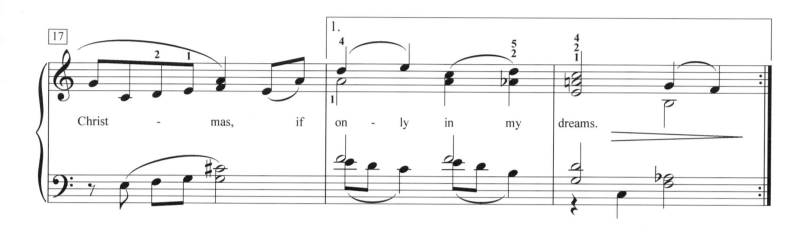

Christ -   mas,   if   on - ly   in my   dreams.

on - ly   in my   dreams.   If   on - ly   in my

dreams.   *rit.*

Have Yourself a Merry Little Christmas

from MEET ME IN ST. LOUIS

Words and Music by Hugh Martin
and Ralph Blane
Arranged by Jennifer and Mike Watts

make the Yule - tide gay. From now on our trou-bles will be miles a -

way. Here we are as in

old - en days, hap - py gold - en days of yore.

Faith - ful friends who are dear to us gath - er near to us once

more.

Through the years we all will be to-geth-er, if the fates al-

low.

Hang a shin-ing star up-on the high-est

bough.

and have your-self

a mer-ry lit-tle Christ-mas now.

The Little Drummer Boy

Words and Music by Harry Simeone,
Henry Onorati and Katherine Davis
Arranged by Jennifer and Mike Watts

fore the King, pa rum pum pum pum, rum pum pum pum, rum pum pum pum,_____

Play R.H. one octave lower to the end

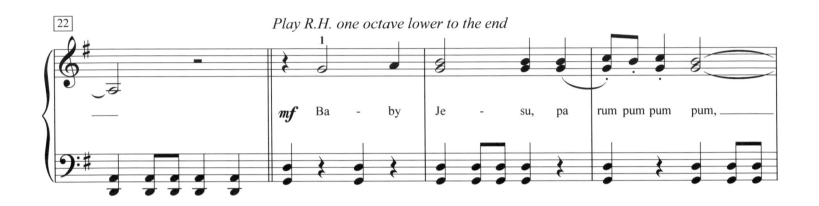

_____ *mf* Ba — by Je — su, pa rum pum pum pum,_____

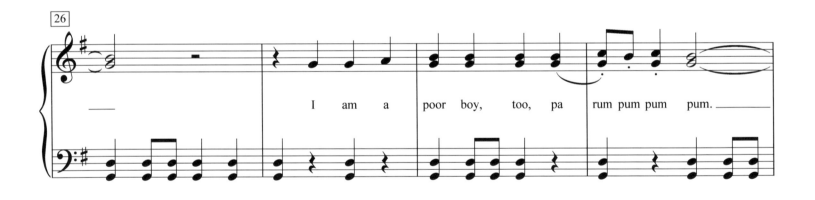

_____ I am a poor boy, too, pa rum pum pum pum._____

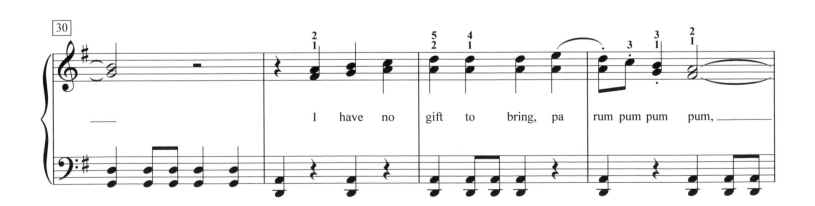

_____ I have no gift to bring, pa rum pum pum pum,_____

Mary's Little Boy Child

Words and Music by
Jester Hairston

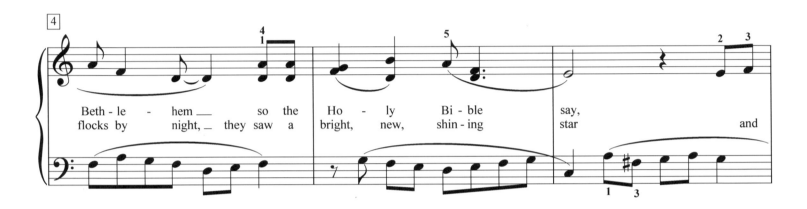

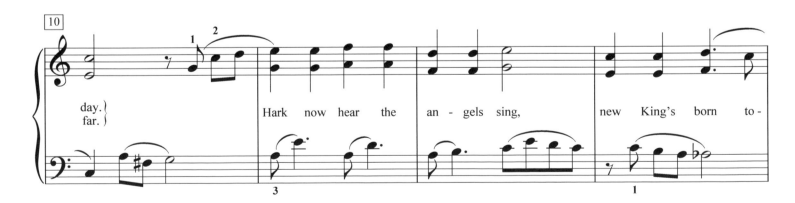

day, and man will live for - ev - er - more ___ be - cause of Christ - mas

1. day. While 2. day. Trum - pets sound and an - gels sing,

Lis - ten to what they say. That man will live for - ev - er - more, ___ be -

cause of Christ - mas day. *rit.*

Little Saint Nick

Words and Music by Brian Wilson
and Mike Love
Arranged by Jennifer and Mike Watts

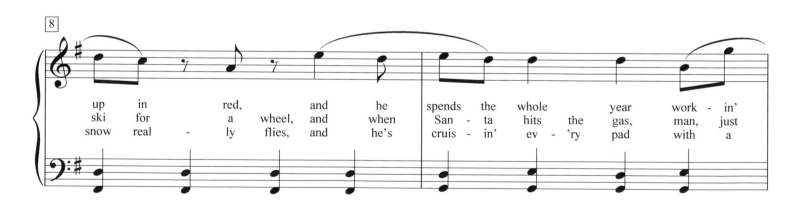

14

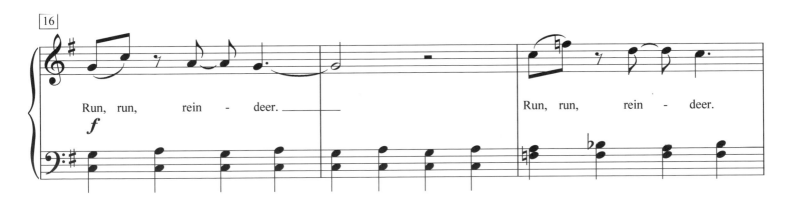

15

Run, run, rein - deer. He don't miss no one. And

Lit - tle Saint Nick. (Lit - tle

Saint Nick.)

The Most Wonderful Time of the Year

Words and Music by Eddie Pola
and George Wyle
Arranged by Jennifer and Mike Watts

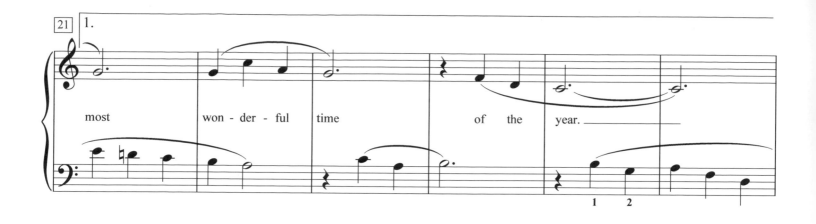

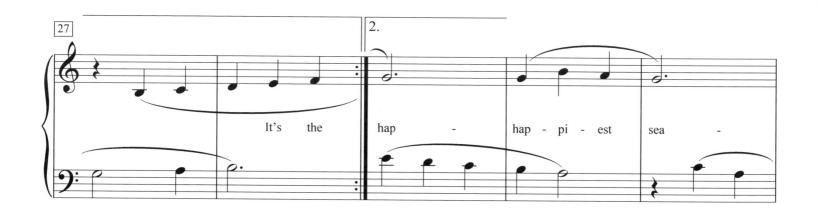

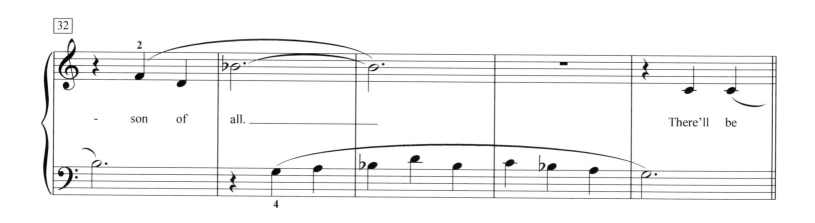

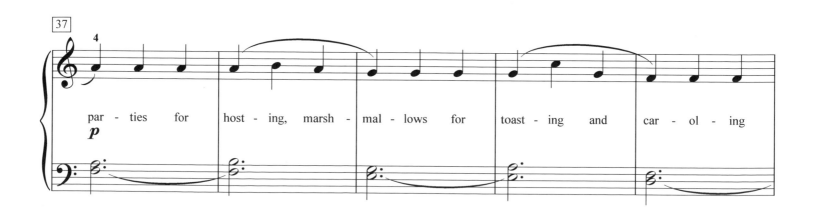

18

out in the snow. There'll be scar - y ghost sto - ries and

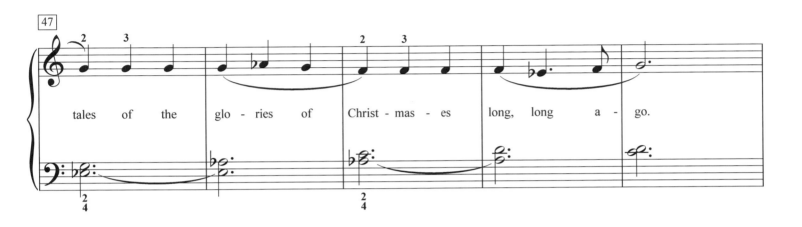

tales of the glo - ries of Christ - mas - es long, long a - go.

D.S. al Coda

CODA

It's the most won - der - ful time of the

year. rit.

19

Winter Wonderland

Words by Dick Smith
Music by Felix Bernard
Arranged by Jennifer and Mike Watts

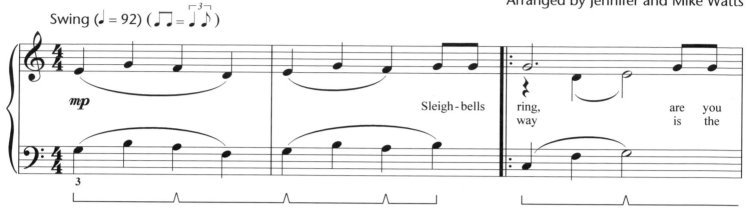

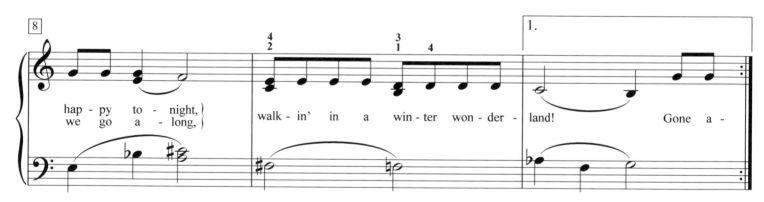

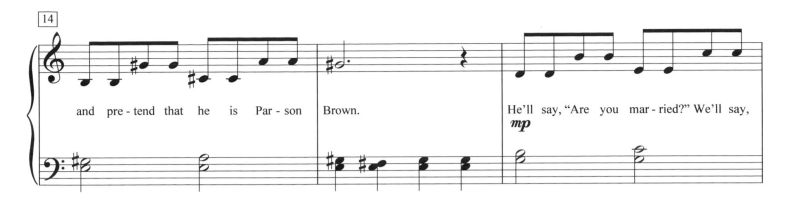

and pre-tend that he is Par - son Brown. He'll say, "Are you mar - ried?" We'll say,

mp

"No, man! But you can do the job when you're in town!" Lat - er on, we'll con-

mf

spire, ___ as we dream by the fire, ___ to face un - a - fraid, the

p

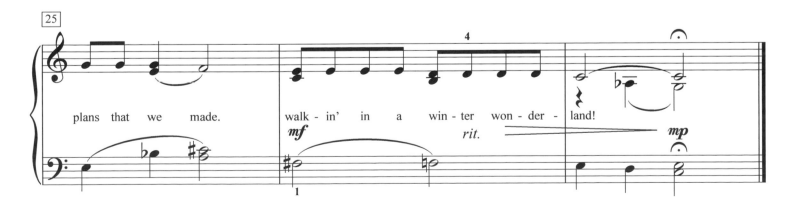

plans that we made. walk - in' in a win - ter won - der - land!

mf *rit.* *mp*

You're a Mean One, Mr. Grinch

Lyrics by Dr. Seuss
Music by Albert Hague
Arranged by Jennifer and Mike Watts

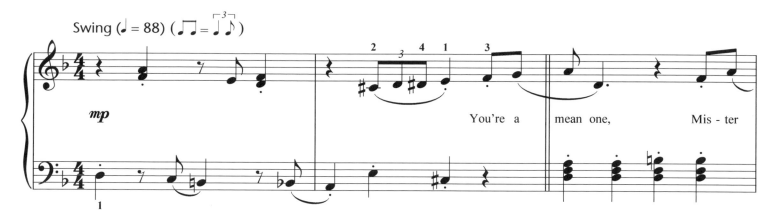

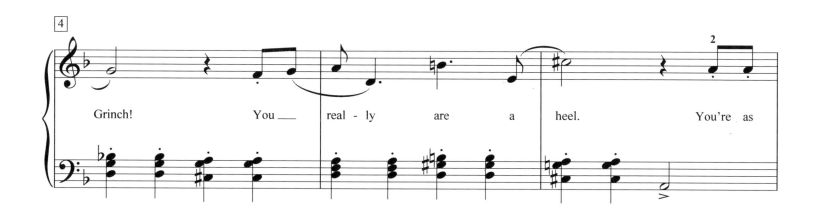

You're a bad ba - nan - a with a greas - y, black peel.

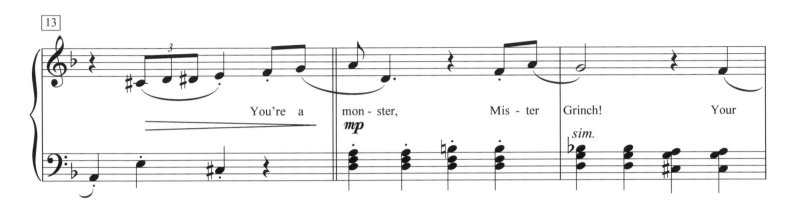

You're a mon - ster, Mis - ter Grinch! Your

heart's an emp - ty hole. Your brain is full of spi - ders, you've got

gar - lic in your soul, Mis - ter Grinch! I would-n't touch you with a

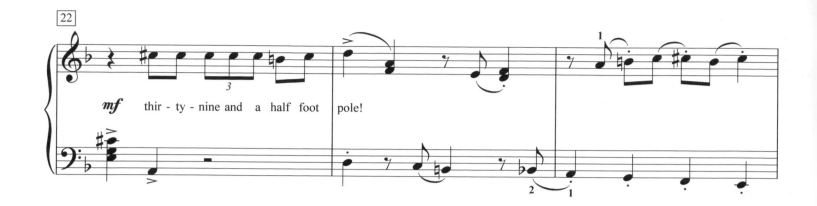

thir - ty - nine and a half foot pole!

Additional Lyrics

3. You're a vile one, Mr. Grinch!
You have termites in your smile.
You have all the tender sweetness
Of a seasick crocodile, Mr. Grinch!
(Spoken:) Given the choice between the two of you,
I'd take the...
(Sung:) seasick crocodile!

4. You're a foul one, Mr. Grinch!
You're a nasty-wasty skunk!
Your heart is full of unwashed socks,
Your soul is full of gunk, Mr. Grinch!
(Spoken:) The three words that best describe you
Are as follows, and I quote:
(Sung:) Stink! Stank! Stunk!

5. You're a rotter, Mr. Grinch!
You're the king of sinful sots.
Your heart's a dead tomato
Spotched with moldy, purple spots, Mr. Grinch!
(Spoken:) Your soul is an appalling dumpheap
overflowing with the most disgraceful assortment of
deplorable rubbish imaginable, mangled up in...
(Sung:) tangled-up knots!

6. You nauseate me, Mr. Grinch!
With a nauseous, super "naus."
You're a crooked jerkey jockey
And you drive a crooked hoss, Mr. Grinch!
(Spoken:) You're a three-decker sauerkraut
and toadstool sandwich...
(Sung:) with arsenic sauce!